JOB COACHING:
THE TOUGHEST JOB
YOU'LL EVER LOVE

Donald Bayne, Sr.

For confidentiality, some names used have been changed.

donbaynejobcoaching@gmail.com

ISBN: **1461001749**
ISBN-13:
978-1461001744

DEDICATION

To those job coaches everywhere who
believe in the people they serve,
even when others may not.

To my wife of 47 years, JoAnn, who
has always believed in me, even
when others did not.

CONTENTS

The real great man is the
man who makes every
man feel great.
-   G. K. Chesterton

1- IGNORE THE VEGETABLES – GO RIGHT FOR THE PIE

Job coaching is hard work, not very glamorous, and at times can wear you down. However the rewards of helping someone to succeed on their job are rewards that will last a lifetime. It's the toughest job you'll ever love.

What we do is to find employment for people with disabilities, and help them to retain those positions. When you meet any new person for the first time and engage them in a conversation, it will probably be less than 5 minutes before the question is asked, "What do you do for a living?" If you have a disability and no employment, how do you answer that question? "I don't have a job, I watch TV." "I play video games all day." Answers like that don't do much for your self-esteem. However, if the answer is:

"I work at a hardware store."

"I'm a custodian."

"I do restaurant work."

"I work at a grocery store."

Do you see what that does? Suddenly, the playing field becomes level. There is an equality to the conversation. A person with a disability who also has a job is someone who has the things that other people have. It gives the person a certain standing, a paycheck, and the ability to purchase things that others have. It says, "I am Somebody."

This is why we work as job coaches. We can help people to have the advantages that other people have. For the client there is the sense of having arrived. For the coach it means having been a part of making this all happen. The feeling is marvelous and the reward cannot be calculated. I suppose that reward can be expressed a thousand different ways but whcn success comes, you'll know how it feels.

I don't want to give you the impression that everything about job coaching is a day at the beach. Sometimes you wonder what you have gotten yourself into. Some days are like eating asparagus. Other days are like eating broccoli. Some days are like eating asparagus AND broccoli. YUCK! There can be disappointments. However, when you see your clients succeeding your day will be like eating a slice of homemade blueberry pie. Other days are like having the entire pie. And, ladies and gentlemen, some weeks are like having the whole pie AND a gallon of ice cream.

So ignore the vegetables – go right for the pie!

2 - LET'S SEE YOUR RESUME'

When I was 14 years old I thought my father was the dumbest man in the world. When I turned 21 I was amazed at how much he had learned in just 7 years.

_____ Mark Twain

Experience – how much does it matter? We know that you can't ever have enough of it. How much do you need to be a job coach? What kinds of experience do you need? It comes in a lot of forms. Here are some of them.

Right away I'd like to know if you've ever worked with people with disabilities. Practical experience like this is very helpful and tells us that you must have enjoyed it or you wouldn't be trying to get this job. You have also shown that you can do the work.

Maybe you have a degree in Human Services. This shows us that you have a desire to do this kind of work, have a natural compassion, a desire to serve others, and have an important knowledge of the system and language of Human Services. That degree is helpful.

What if you have neither work experience nor a degree? Remain seated, you're still in the game. Do you have a relative or a friend with a disability? Years of interaction with such a person goes a long way toward training you to be a job coach. You have a unique perspective that few people possess.

Maybe you have a disability yourself. This will give you greater understanding of the people we support and help to make you a solid job coach.

All right, we've examined four types of experience and maybe you don't fit any of them. Still, you may possess important qualities that will make you a good job coach. Let's call this category, "Nuts and Bolts". Do you have people skills? Do you have good common sense? Can you place yourself in the shoes of other people and think the way *they* think? If you have these qualities then you have tools that every job coach needs. Finally, do you know what it feels like to have suffered adversity? Do you know how it feels to *overcome* adversity? If your answer is yes, this will also help you to identify with people who have disabilities. A degree from the School of Hard Knocks is always welcome in the world of job coaching.

So now you've been hired. You may have lots of experience, you may have little. Every new coach hired means a new set of eyes that may see things in a client that the rest of us haven't. You may be very young and not have a wealth of experience but have enough enthusiasm to set the building on fire. Or you may have built up a wealth of common sense over the years.

Will you make mistakes? Yes. But years from now you will have cut down on them but you will still make them. This is a difficult job, folks. Much of it is very unscientific. There are no templates because each person we support has different needs. Just remember this: don't let anyone criticize you because you are young or because you are inexperienced. You are just learning, the way the rest of us are *still* learning and along the way you will make discoveries that will teach the rest of us.

3 - MY MOTHER THE DETECTIVE

All right, who did it?
                    ___ Any person who has ever
                    raised children.

When I was growing up I had reason to believe that my mother must have been a detective sometime before I was born. She always seemed to be able to figure out when I had done something I shouldn't have done. She had few rules but made sure they were enforced. Such as:

- Wipe your feet before you track snow or mud across the floor.
- Don't snitch desserts out of the refrigerator or the cookie jar.
- Don't throw the ball in the house.

The first rule was rational. The second was unpleasant. The third was unconstitutional. In order to break the third rule you had to have a second person participate. For a brief period of my young life I had a step brother living with us but otherwise I was an only child. He was 3 years older than me, and, I thought, smarter and wiser.

When I was 8 years old my mother left my stepbrother and me by ourselves while she went down the street to go grocery shopping. All by ourselves in the house – talk about temptation. You have to understand what it meant to be a boy in a major league city in those days. Kids thought that baseball was life itself. Even the dogs barked baseball. My mother knew nothing about baseball. She didn't know Henry Aaron from Henry Longfellow. It was winter and below freezing outside. We just had to throw a baseball in the house. We were having a great time tossing one back and forth when the following sequence occurred:

Throw

  Miss

    Crash

    Trouble

The ball had hit an 8 X 10 picture and sent it crashing to the floor. We were dead meat. However, my older, smarter, wiser step-brother had a plan. He reasoned that if we removed the broken glass from the frame and took it outside to the trash can we'd never get caught. The frame and the picture were undamaged. We would just put it back where it had been, it would look the same, and no one would know the difference. What a great idea! Well, my mother arrived home from shopping. She wasn't back 5 minutes when she asked, "What happened to the glass in that picture?"

I threw myself on the mercy of the court.

How in the world did she know? I told you she was a detective. Looking back, I've figured out how she did it. In fact, I used her methods when I raised my own children. She was familiar with her surroundings, in this case her house. She knew the circumstances – cold weather and an unsupervised atmosphere. Then there were those boys and their unusual (for her) love of baseball. Finally, she knew a guilty look when she saw one, and rounded up the usual suspects.

Job coaching is a lot like that. It is detective work and problem solving. We are constantly trying to solve cases like these:

- What kind of job can we find for a person whose support needs make it difficult to find employment?
- Why is our client suddenly having behavioral issues?
- How do we convince an employer to hire our people?
- How do we solve client transportation problems when a bus route is altered or a shift is changed to later at night?
- Can a certain job be performed by someone in a wheel chair and how do we convince an employer that it can?

Job coaches face these situations all the time. How do we solve them? The first thing we must do is to get to know the person we are supporting. This is an open and shut case. We need to keep our eyes open and our mouths shut. Get to know your client through observation. Sure, you need to engage in conversation, but let the other person talk. You will learn a lot of things which will prove important later on when a crisis comes along.

Next, develop a network of people who know your client. The more interest you show in your client the more interest others will show in aiding the development of the person you are supporting. Contact the people who are close to her/him. Maybe it's a caregiver or a relative. It's amazing how much they want to share information with you. They have a stake in the person's life, too. Maybe this person has been served by your agency for a long time. Try talking to other job coaches who have previously worked with this person. They can be great sources also.

Other relevant information can come from the written word. Read the information in the person's file. The psychological evaluation may be helpful. So can past goal plans, person centered plans, NISH evaluations, and incident reports. I once found a job for a man because I found an interest of his which matched a particular position available. I found that information buried in a 5 year old person centered plan. Also, take the time to go back through old log/case notes. You may find out what works and what doesn't about a person. There may be a past behavioral issue in there that will shed some light on what is happening right now. Any of these sources might tip you off to a problem you might be having. For instance, why does a particular person exhibit a certain behavior only occasionally, and not at other times. Your network of people close to the client, or perhaps through that paper trail, may indicate that this action is a sure sign of anxiety, for instance.

Finally, it is helpful to educate yourself about particular disabilities. You can talk to others who know, you can read books or use the internet to learn about autism, Down syndrome, epilepsy, anxiety disorders and other mental illnesses, and cerebral palsy, to name a few. Every one of the sources mentioned in this chapter can help you to better support your client.

You have been given some ideas on how to look for answers. Let's look at some common puzzles we face that need to be solved:

- A woman who has been stable on a job for 2 years suddenly has attendance problems.
- A man known for his politeness is suddenly disrespectful to his supervisor.
- A new hire with some experience in 2 previous jobs is doing poorly in the third job in a similar profession. She shows no attention to the detail required and doesn't seem to care.

How do we figure out what's going on? Let's start by asking 2 questions. First, "What has changed in this person's life?" This is where the detective work begins. The answer could be one of a thousand things. This is where your network of information can help you out. By talking to relatives, caregivers, other coaches, etc., you might find the answer, which is not always obvious. Here are some common questions to ask:

- Has there been a change in medications?
- Does the person have a new physical problem?
- Is there a new caregiver?

- Is there a new living situation? New residence? New roommate?
- Has a loss occurred? A relative? A pet? A possession?
- Does the person have a new supervisor? New co-worker(s)?
- Has the work schedule changed and is it causing the loss of a favorite activity?
- Does the person miss the previous job coach?
- Has a work, home, or transportation routine changed?
- Has spending money been reduced for any reason?

Those are 10 questions you might ask. There are only 990 other things you might think of. Once you come upon the right question you will be closer to figuring out how to solve the problem. Remember, change can have a negative impact on everything you do, whether you are disabled or non-disabled.

The other question to ask comes in 3 parts, is pretty obvious, and often gets overlooked. They are:

- Does the person want this job?
- Does the person want ANY job?

- Does the job coach want the person to have this job more than the client wants this job?

Does your client want this job? Well, have you ever had a job you didn't like even if you liked it for a while – maybe a few months or even a few years?

Does the person want ANY job? Lots of people choose retirement every day. Some people don't like to work at any age. Do you think you can change this? Good luck.

Does the coach want the person to have this job more than the client wants this job? I once had a man on my custodial crew who had failed on every job he had ever had. After two months on my crew he became the best custodian I had. He loved his work, I gave him more and more responsibility, and he was free to be himself. Now in his mid-thirties he was suddenly a success. A year later our staff thought that it was time for him to get a job in the community. We set up an interview at a fast food restaurant, got him to wear some good clothes, and tidied up his hair. He got the job and everyone was happy – or so we thought. Pretty soon we started getting reports back of inappropriate behavior, careless language, and poor hygiene and dress habits. He was eventually fired and came back to working on the crew. He flourished just as he had before.

What went wrong? Well, the staff wanted him to have the fast food job much more than the client wanted it. No one really asked him what he wanted. The lesson is to not put people in the wrong job just because there is an opening, or just because YOU think this is the right job for someone. Twenty years later I still think of that mistake.

The right kind of detective work can help you to find answers to solve some work problems your client may be experiencing. But, what do you do when all your research still doesn't give you the answers? Let's move on to the next chapter to find out.

4 - THE BRAIN BEHIND YOUR SMILE

Real thinking is hard work, which is why so very few people ever do any of it.
                    ___Winston Churchill

All right, you're stuck. You've tried everything you know of to solve the kinds of problems mentioned in the previous chapter, the kinds we encounter all the time. Still, you haven't figured out what to do. You've reached a dead end. Now what? Well, that's why we hired you. You can't solve every puzzle but you can solve many just by *thinking*.

Gathering information, as we have seen, depends on picking other people's brains. This is true teamwork and a real sight to behold when it is working. Real thinking, however, is a lonelier route and depends on *YOU*, not just on others. How good a coach you become depends on how well you commit yourself to independent thinking.

Dreamers solve the world's problems. They don't know it can't be done so they go out and do it. ___Bill Veeck

Veeck was a dreamer and a promoter. He owned baseball teams in the middle of the last century and everywhere he went he boosted attendance because of his stunts and giveaways that brought more people to the ballpark. Everyone does it now but in the 1940's and 1950's no one had ever heard of Fireworks Night, Bat Day, free prizes, or any of that, as a way to draw larger crowds. He was way ahead of his time and he was a dreamer.

Dreamers are fairly easy to spot. They tend to bump into you in the hallway or to stare off into space. They generally fall into 3 categories.

The first can be found sitting at a desk with their smile upside down. They are wearing a frown and have a general aura of sadness about them. Life can be hard on all of us and we all know how that feels. This kind of dreaming goes inward and emphasizes our personal problems, which doesn't always lead to productive thinking. This kind of dreamer is not the one we are interested in.

The second has a different look. The mouth now is turned into a half smile, a really satisfied look, and their eyes are half closed. There's no doubt about it, this person has recently fallen in love. That isn't the dreamer we are looking for, either.

The third is just staring – no frown, no smile – just staring. This is the dreamer that is working on an idea and the person who solves problems – my kind of job coach.

History is filled with people in this third category. They are people who think – *hard*. They ask the question, "I wonder what would happen if I tried *this*?" Name a profession and there were great women and men within that group that asked that question. For instance, "I wonder if the earth is round and revolves around the sun?" "I wonder what would happen if we took a virus that causes a disease and use it to make a vaccine to prevent that disease?" "I wonder if a car could run on electricity instead of gasoline?" "I wonder if people with developmental disabilities could hold a job and make contributions to society?" Throughout history people have asked the right questions to find the right answers.

So how do we implement the kind of thinking which solves problems and changes people's lives? I can hear it now, "I don't have time to do this kind of thinking! My case load is overwhelming, I'm behind on my paperwork, I need more time for job development, and I'm so busy I had to ask someone else to eat my lunch for me – I didn't have time."

We all have these feelings at times. So what's the answer? Well, it's up to you to create thinking time. Do you ever have to drive a few miles and have nothing else to do? Turn off the radio and think. Do you ever get into a boring situation which requires no thinking? THINK! I'm sure we would like to do our thinking at work and when we leave work – we *leave* work. If that sentence describes you, please don't read the next one. I said don't... Okay, go ahead and read it. I happen to walk on a treadmill every night. It's boring and monotonous so I have plenty of time to think. Many of the thoughts in this book came out of my treadmill experience.

My son likes to think and plan while playing video games, and has done that for almost 30 years. That doesn't work for me but it does for him. Walking in the woods is much more effective for me. Maybe a lake or an ocean outing works for you. I even know a former supervisor of mine who got good ideas from dreaming at night. It doesn't matter how you do it, but to be a good job coach you have to be a thinker.

Along with thinking comes good intuition. I've known dozens of job coaches in my life. Some were very good, some were great, and the rest are doing something else for a living right now. Every good job coach I've ever met has had good intuition for coaching. This is true for all professions. Mechanics, nurses, teachers, scientists, warehouse managers, politicians, custodians, carpenters, public speakers, auto sales persons, people who fish, you name it. If they are any good at what they do, they have good intuition for the things that happen in their trade.

Can intuition be explained? I'm not sure but I'll give it a try. When you have a little knowledge of something it seems to help trigger intuitive thoughts. You take what you know and use it to help you find what you don't know. You solve a problem and someone asks, "How did you figure that out?" Your answer is, "I can't explain it – I just knew."

- Intuition.
- Gut feeling.
- It just seemed right.

These are all ways of expressing the same thing. Major decisions are made every day in our world because people use their intuition. Their intuitive talent works for them. Some are good only within their professions. Believe me, brain surgeons don't call me when they have a problem. They use their knowledge and their intuition to figure out problems. By the same token most people in other professions couldn't do our job successfully. Good job coaches have a special talent and intuitive skills that others don't possess.

Real thinking and the use of intuitive skills are qualities that lead to success for the coach which will lead to success for your clients. I'll wrap this up with a story I once read about Dr. Richard Feynmann. He was a physicist who worked on the Manhattan Project which developed the atomic bomb. His later work in physics was universally known throughout the science world. He was also a key member of the commission that investigated the Challenger space disaster. When he was a teenager during the Great Depression he earned money because he had a talent for repairing radios. One day he was in a customer's home and the owner found Feynmann sitting at the table staring at the radio.

"What are you doing", said the owner.
"I'm thinking", said Feynmann.
The owner called out to his wife, "Hey Mabel, this boy fixes radios just by thinking."

It's a lesson we all could learn.

If we wonder often the gift of knowledge will come. ___Arapaho proverb

5 - THE SMILE IN FRONT OF YOUR BRAIN

The easiest part of my job is to be nice to people. ___Richard Petty

When I first entered residential work for people with developmental disabilities I got some great advice from the program manager. They once had a residential caregiver who had an unpleasant life away from the job and brought her problems to work with her every day. She would enter her client's apartment with a look on her face that might indicate that she had just finished killing snakes. Frown and a half. One day the client decided she'd had enough of this negative attitude. When the worker showed up looking sour the client threw a shoe at her. The lesson was to start your day with a positive look and a positive attitude.

Your client will respond to whatever attitude you bring to work.

Think about some tough days you've had. You overslept and had to miss breakfast. You get to work, check your email, and are informed that there is a problem with one of your clients. Then you spill coffee all over your desk. It's 9:30 in the morning and you have a client coming in 10 minutes. Are you going to meet her with a smile or are you going to drag your problems along with you? Your client deserves the smile. The choice is yours.

This is easy for some people. They seem to smile and be upbeat all the time. Nothing seems to rattle them. However, for the rest of us, we sometimes have to work at it when we are having ONE OF THOSE DAYS. I look at it this way. If we want our clients to succeed it is up to the job coach to create a positive work atmosphere. People perform better when they are happy and it is up to us to see that this happens.

How you do this depends on your individual style and personality. We are all different, but there are some general principles we all can use. For instance, treat people the way you want to be treated. All of us understand that and all of us can do it.

So, how do you treat people? Or, how do YOU treat people? When you are carrying on a conversation with another adult you just naturally use a normal tone of voice. Do you use that same tone of voice when speaking to a person with a developmental disability? You had better! It comes across clearly that you are looking down on somebody when you speak to them as if you were speaking to a child. Do you want a person to act like an adult and perform like an adult on the job? Then treat people like adults.

How do you address someone? By the adult name that that person has chosen for herself/himself. Ask them what they would like to be called. Many of us chose our adult name. When I was maybe 12 or 13, I wanted to be called Don instead of Donnie. Maybe that happened to you, too. It is certainly inappropriate for any person to call a co-worker honey, dear, or sweetheart. Unfortunately, I have seen some job coaches put on their best baby voices and address a client as "honey", or some other degrading thing. Why not just say, "Hi, Infant, how are you doing?"

So, you've reported for work with a smile on your face. You've addressed your client and treated that person as an adult. Now it is time to go to the job site for that person's first day on the job.

Take along a mental checklist for yourself. First, put yourself in your client's shoes. A new job means change, and a new job means that there is a possibility of failure. There are a small percentage of people who are just bubbling with confidence with each new challenge that comes along, but for the rest of us the change and failure ghosts can haunt us. This is where every person you will ever serve needs a good dose of positive reinforcement. Stop and think about what happens to a new employee's confidence when the job coach's first response is negative. You can boost someone's confidence by teaching that person correctly so that the first response CAN be positive.

The idea of positive reinforcement is crucial to your client's success. Many clients are told throughout their lives that they are inferior in one way or another. A person has not been in school very long before they realize that they are already behind the other students. They develop a reputation as being "different". They are generally unable to achieve the customary expectations in reading or math, athletics, speech, or to obtain things like a driver's license. Now they are adults and how will they achieve success on the job? Look, we all need to be valued, we all need to feel like we are SOMEBODY.

This is where a good job coach comes in. You know, the one with the smile. Show the person what they are doing right. They've had a lifetime of being shown what they do wrong. Believe in them – believe that they can succeed. Don't give false praise – that is condescending. Watch for the good things and point them out. When a person succeeds at one thing, it is easier for them to believe they can succeed at others.

That smile you are wearing affects more than just the people you serve. It goes with you to the job sites as well. When initial contact is made with a potential employer, are they seeing in you someone they would like to do business with? Do they feel the passion in your presentation that makes them think that you strongly believe in people with disabilities? When those answers are "yes" you've gone a long way towards getting someone a job, and it doesn't end there. The job may involve your client working with non-disabled co-workers. It will benefit your client if you make friends with their supervisor and other people that they work with. When this is done you will find these groups of people making a greater effort to see that your client succeeds. You can't make too many friends.

I want to conclude this section with two personal experiences I've had which show how important it is that we project the proper image toward the people we serve. Both of them involve hospitalizations. The first came when I was 3 years old to remove my tonsils. In those days tonsils were not so much considered a body part as they were a disease to be cured by removal. Besides, you could then put them under your pillow and the Tonsil Fairy would leave you a quarter. It was the policy of hospitals then to check you in on the day before the surgery, a practice that continued until the insurance companies got tired of paying for the extra day and people then reported on the day of surgery.

I was stuck with the old way of doing things. So, my parents brought me in and left that evening when told to do so. Now here I am, 3 years old, lying in a crib, never having been away from home overnight, and barely understanding what was going on. After what seemed like an hour of lying in this crib, a nurse comes in, turns out the light, and says, "Be quiet and go to sleep!" It was an unkind way to treat a scared and confused child. You have to wonder why she became a pediatric nurse in the first place.

Now let's move ahead 61 years to another surgery. I had to have open heart surgery which turned out to be more serious than expected. By the time I woke up and could make sense of things over 24 hours later there were tubes and wires and hospital machinery everyplace. I had a lot of support from people close to me. Visitors came in the daytime, and my family members were always around during the day and evening. But people have to sleep sometime so it was that period from about 10pm to 6am when I was alone – and often not sleeping. I was sick, I was scared, and I was pretty much helpless. The only people I saw during those hours were the nurses and nurse's assistants. As I laid there wide awake they would peek their head in frequently. Sometimes they were checking vital signs or giving injections. Other times they just wanted to make sure I was all right. I needed more than medicine – I needed reassurance and care and they gave it to me. They truly were angels and I owe them so much. As my 9 days of hospitalization progressed I started to tell them individually how much it meant to me to see a friendly face. Those faces and the care they represented were crucial to my physical and emotional healing.

I've thought about those nurses and the importance of the friendly face almost every day since then. It proves what I've always believed about job coaching. Many of the people we serve know what the UN-friendly face has looked like in their lives. It could be a relative, a teacher, a caregiver, a previous employer, a co-worker, a neighbor, etc. What they should remember about you is that you are one of the people who had the friendly face, the one that makes their working experience and their life a whole lot better.

6 - IT'S WHAT YOU LEARN AFTER YOU KNOW IT ALL THAT COUNTS

Major League manager Earl Weaver was right when he made the above statement. As long as you are a job coach you will never quit learning. If I were to write this book five years from now it would be a longer book because I would have learned more things to write about. This chapter will touch on several things that coaches experience.

Here's a question for you. What do you do for a living?

Here are some answers:

- I'm a job coach.
- I'm a job trainer.
- I work with people with disabilities.
- I'm in human services.
- I'm an employment specialist.

Any of those answers describe what you do. Here's another answer:

- I teach.

Correct. We all teach, and how we teach will determine how successful our clients will become. If you are going to *teach*, then it is vital to know how people *learn*. The answers to how people learn are numerous and it is up to you to figure out how. Generally, I find it is easier to show someone how to do something than it is to just tell them – or a combination of showing them while also talking to them at the same time. Why do I think this is best? Because that is how I learn the best. That oral stuff doesn't work for me. For instance, let's start with that incorrect phrase, "Easy to assemble". You read the instructions (written by someone who assembles these gadgets all the time). Guess what? It isn't easy after all. Easy would mean that the gadget comes with a real person to show you how to do it.

I can remember having several teachers in elementary school who would read something to the class for about 5 minutes and then ask questions about what was just read. After about the first 30 seconds of this reading I'd be staring out the window or day dreaming because I couldn't concentrate. Then I would try to hide behind whoever was sitting in front of me and hope that I wouldn't be called upon to answer any questions.

So find out how people learn things and then begin to teach. Ask yourself, "How do I learn". That will help. But remember that we are all different and have different ways of learning. The most important thing is not how I learn, but how my client learns.

What do you do when you are coaching someone and you are not having success? Do you keep doing the same things over and over? Who told you that that would work? I previously stated that it is a good idea to talk to other people who know your client to get some good ideas. This will always be true. However, you have to be careful not to get outdated or inaccurate information. What may have been true about someone in 1994 may not be true in 2011. People change their tastes, their behavior, and they mature. Be sure that your information is accurate and up to date.

In 1994 I was a big fan of the San Francisco Giants, ate a lot of desserts, wore thick glasses, and owned an antique store. None of these things are true today. It is out of date information. So, if you are following someone else's advice or your own ideas for a period of time and it isn't working, SCRAP IT, and try something else. The definition of foolishness is to try something 16 times and failing, then trying the same thing the same way a 17th time expecting a different outcome.

Expect that each client you work with will know something that you don't know. I've worked with dozens of people with disabilities and every person had some knowledge that I didn't possess. I once met a man with many support needs who would ask people their birth date. After receiving the date he would then tell them the day of the week on which they were born. He never missed. (For those of you who are taking notes, he told me I was born on Wednesday.)

I've also known people with developmental disabilities who knew more than I did about:

- The long history of professional wrestling.

- Painting beautiful pictures.
- Pop culture.
- World War Two.
- Fishing.
- ...and 2000 other things.

I once supervised a work crew that was responsible for the washing of all 12 of the agency's transportation vans. We had to park them in a certain spot so that the hose would reach all the way around the vehicle. Behind the right rear wheel was a pothole that was always filling up with water, was a nuisance, and we always had to step around it. Like some other things in all of our lives, I never got around to doing anything about it.

One day we received a request to dispose of some clumps of sod which were created when a group of people started a garden. We had the time so we grabbed a wheelbarrow, filled it with sod, and headed for the dumpster. We started tossing sod in the trash when Bill, a member of the crew said, "Why don't we put some of this sod in that pothole?" Brilliant! Here the agency was paying me to solve problems like that and Bill winds up solving it for me. Don't underestimate the people you are serving.

I believe that we should have high expectations in regard to our clients. High expectations are not the same as unrealistic expectations. It is, however, a wonderful thing to see a talent in someone – a talent that others do not see, and possibly a talent not seen by the person themself. We can encourage people to go beyond where they are now.

Shoot for the moon. Even if you miss, you will land among the stars.
___Anonymous

(Boy, that Anonymous person sure said a lot of smart things.)

In California, I supervised a custodial crew of developmentally disabled adults. While working for this agency I had the opportunity to encounter a man named Phillip. It was easy to spot him. He was always talking, loud, a know-it-all, and often borderline obnoxious. Staff members avoided him when possible because they knew that once engaged, they would never get away from him. I got to know him and I'll have to admit that he could be difficult. But on a couple of occasions I mentioned in passing to staff members that I thought Phillip could succeed on our custodial crew. These statements were met with looks of disbelief. Months later, somebody took me up on it and Phillip became a member of our crew. I'm sure there was some background laughter during the meeting that produced that decision.

On his first night, before he started work, I sat down and talked with him. I told him that working with us would be nothing like the day program in which he had been involved. That had been more like school, with craft classes, fun, treats, and games. I told him that what he would be doing was a job and that we had high standards. For instance, when it is break time you talk – when it is work time you work. Phillip learned to do just that. His productivity was a little slow but the results were perfect. He was always on time and never missed work. His stamina increased and his productivity picked up. There were a couple of behavioral incidents but we worked them out. Things were going well.

About 4 months after he started, his case manager called for his annual

Individual Service Plan meeting to be held at his group home. Present were his parents, group home director, case manager, a couple of people from programs in which he was involved, Phillip himself, and me. We sat around a huge dining room table. The meeting started with comments from each individual, beginning with his parents. They just trashed him. Then everyone else picked up the ball and found something about him to criticize. I suspected that some of these things had happened long ago and were not current information. The last person on the trip around the table was me. I began by saying that it was hard to believe that we were all speaking about the same person. I said that Phillip was giving me all that I had asked of him. He was out of shape when he started but that his stamina was improving. I no longer had to check his work because he was doing things correctly. He had become a valuable member of the crew.

This speech was followed by dead silence in the room. After all the criticism, what could anyone say? They just stared at me like I was an outsider. It was the look that says, "You were invited to the party and you dumped vinegar in the punch".

I could only imagine how Phillip felt. He had found the friendly face. He realized that somebody believed in him and he produced because of it.

Not all stories end this way. You can have high expectations of everyone yet some people won't succeed. BUT SOME PEOPLE WILL! It is your job to see that as many people as possible are given the opportunity to make it. To be sure that success takes place, let's review:

- Get to know your client.
- Do the detective work.
- Use your brain when you get stuck.
- Create the friendly face.
- Believe in people – believe that they are going to make it.

If you do these things, I guarantee – GUARANTEE – the more cooperation you are going to get, the better job people will do, the more their self-image will improve, and the more smiles you are going to see. And one of those smiles is going to be yours. Oh, and the happier and more fulfilled you will be.

When you go home at night you'll know that when you've done your job that you have helped to make a difference in someone's life, that you've done something *important*. It's the toughest job you'll ever love.

7 - TRAINING SESSIONS

This section is written for job coach trainers and managers. The following exercises are designed to help your job coaches become even better at their jobs.

Sometime during a staff meeting, or a time set aside to train job coaches, your agency might consider the following exercises.

EXERCISE #1
TESTING YOUR I.Q.

Ask your group the following ten questions. No one can look up the answer. Have them write their answers on a piece of paper.

1. What is a bubbler?
2. What is a sugarbush?
3. What is a paddle pop?

4. Who was Nippy Jones, and what did he do to make himself so famous? Be specific.
5. What does it mean to "peel popple"?
6. What is a Henry J?
7. What is Univac?
8. What do these three words have in common? Tomahawk, Wauwatosa and Oconomowoc.
9. Camp David, in Maryland, has been a presidential retreat since 1953. Why is it called Camp David?
10. After they had been in business for 11 years, this company decided to use the medium of television to advertise its product, in 1950. The advertising slogan was, "More bounce to the ounce." What was that product?

The Answers:

1. A drinking fountain in Wisconsin
2. A grove of sugar maple trees that produce the sap from which pure maple syrup is made.
3. An ice cream bar
4. Nippy Jones was a journeyman baseball player. In Game Four of the 1957 World Series he came up to bat in the tenth inning for the Milwaukee Braves, trailing the New York Yankees,

5-4. He was hit on the foot by a pitch, but the umpire didn't believe him. The ball was retrieved and a smudge of black shoe polish was found on the ball. He went to first base. This became the famous "shoe polish" incident, which started a game winning rally which led to the Braves eventually winning the World Series that year.

5. Poplar trees are cut down at a certain time in the summer when the bark is easy to peel off. School kids used to make money peeling the bark in the summer. The logs were then sent to mills to make paper.

6. A Henry J. was a car made in the early 1950s by the Henry J. Kaiser Corporation. The car looked like something George Jetson might drive. It didn't sell well at all so Kaiser went back to selling aluminum foil and cement and eventually started the Kaiser HMO.

7. Univac stands for "Universal Automatic Computer". It was put on the market in 1951 and used to call the 1952 presidential election results on CBS. It was the first commercial computer and was generally known as an "electronic brain". It weighed

several tons and took up an entire room. Times have changed.

8. They are all cities in Wisconsin.

9. It was named for David Eisenhower, President Eisenhower's grandson. Years later, David married Julie Nixon, daughter of President Richard Nixon.

10. Pepsi. After years of modest sales Pepsi Cola became the number 2 selling soft drink in the country, behind only Coca Cola – today they are number 1.

Multiply the number of correct answers by 15. Now what if I told you this was your I.Q.? You would be insulted and cry foul. The only way you could answer all of these questions correctly is to be raised WHERE I was raised and WHEN I was raised. That would be in the state of Wisconsin in the 1950s. It would be unfair to call this your I.Q. because I'd be using unfamiliar terms and sort of speaking a foreign language.

The question, then, for job coaches is, "Why do we sometimes speak a language that our clients don't understand?" Let's consider the words we often use to communicate directly with our clients. How about this one: inappropriate behavior.

Does everyone you work with understand that? One time at a meeting with staff and a client, I used the word, "entail". I realized immediately that the man did not understand and I rephrased the sentence.

We tend to use Human Service terms because they are familiar to us or we've heard other coaches use them. You could work in Human Services in Tennessee or New York and then move to the state of Washington and be completely confused. Here, as elsewhere we like to use initials. On your first day on the job in Washington would you be able to properly identify DDD, TWE, DVR, DSHS or APS?

We need to speak in terms that our clients will understand. You don't need to treat them like children. Just put yourself in their place. All the teaching efforts in the world will fail if the recipient doesn't understand the language you are speaking. Sure, I know it's English, but some of our speech contains terms that are lost on our clients and that doesn't just include those for whom English is a second language. I'll show you what I mean. We were once having an ongoing discipline problem with a young man and it finally reached the point where we called a meeting involving me, the man, his crew supervisor, and his parents. I opened the meeting by saying something like, " Bob, we are not here to bawl you out, we are here because we want to see you succeed". Simple, honest, and well put, or so I thought. The meeting eventually ended and a week later his crew supervisor said to me that Bob had a question for her: "What does Don mean when he says 'succeed'? It didn't occur to me that that I was speaking a language he couldn't understand. Be sure that you are communicating.

EXERCISE#2
HOW DOES IT FEEL TO HAVE A DISABILITY?

To effectively work with people who have disabilities, you have to understand what it feels like to have certain limitations. The following seven exercises will help you and your staff to develop that understanding. Here we will walk in the other person's shoes and see through their eyes.

FIRST EXERCISE

Have the following items ready before the session starts

- 25 pieces of paper cut into approximately 1"x1" squares and put into a small envelope
- Four or five envelopes, each with 25 pieces of paper, so that more than one staff member does this exercise.
- Four or five pairs of heavy work gloves

Before giving out anything to the staff members, or showing them the gloves, demonstrate with your own set of papers by first emptying one of the envelopes (with your bare hands). Place the papers in five rows across and five rows down until you have a square formation of the 25 pieces of paper. It took me about 40 seconds to complete the demonstration.

Now pass out envelopes to those chosen to do the exercise, and instruct them to duplicate what you have done – then pass out the work gloves and tell them they will be wearing the gloves for this exercise. I guarantee that it will take much more than 40 seconds as they struggle to separate the tiny squares and they will drop them while trying to complete the task.

The purpose of this exercise is to show staff members what it feels like to have poor fine motor skills. Your agency may have clients with cerebral palsy, or other disabilities which could affect their hands and make everyday tasks difficult because of their disability.

SECOND EXERCISE

You will need a radio or CD player and something descriptive to read (either from a book or write your own text). I chose to describe the first car I ever owned. The reading should take about 30 seconds.

Instruct the staff to listen carefully to the words you are about to read because you are going to question them about it when you are done. Now it gets interesting. At the very moment that you begin reading, turn the radio or CD player on. Have it tuned in advance so it is about the same volume or a little louder than your voice.

I chose an exciting football highlight for my presentation and had it programmed to start as soon as I pushed the button and started reading.

When questioned after the reading, only one staff member got all the details of the reading correct. The recording caused too much interference for most to be able to follow the reading. This is what it feels like to have a mental illness that causes a person to hear voices. It is sometimes difficult, and at other times impossible, to follow a conversation. The voices are competing with the people who are talking to you. Now you can have at least some idea what that feels like.

THIRD EXERCISE

You will need a handful of foreign coins, some metal slugs or tokens. When I did this I used pesos and Canadian coins mixed. Pass a handful of coins out to some staff members and ask them to count out 83 cents. They of course won't be able to do it. This is what life would be like if you were unable to count. It reduces the number of jobs you can perform and makes you dependent on the honesty of every store clerk you encounter to charge you the correct amount and give you the correct amount of change. What would that do to your self-image?

FOURTH EXERCISE

You will need a heavy box. I used a box full of heavy file folders. It needs to be heavy enough to be an effort to carry, but not so heavy as to cause a back injury. You know what a Workers Compensation claim could do to your agency's budget. Place the box out of sight of the staff, somewhere in the building or room.

I chose a young person and said "This will be easy, all you have to do is keep up with me on a walk today", (I am a considerably older person). So in the presence of the staff, we took off across the building, just walking, carrying nothing, so it appeared it wouldn't be hard to keep up with me.

On the way around the building we stopped and I had him pick up the heavy box and we made a couple laps of the building (if you are in a large room you can make circuits of the room). As you walk, steadily increase your speed and if necessary, add a few books to the box to make it increasingly hard to carry. It should become increasingly difficult for the box carrier to keep up, and at the end of the tests your carrier will be winded and glad to set the box down, which they have not been allowed to do during the exercise.

It seems that all of us have a client who cannot walk fast or keep up with us. It could be because of a disability with a leg that doesn't work properly. It could be a breathing or stamina problem. Maybe it is a body size problem, or perhaps it is someone that is aging. Be sensitive to these things because their lives are like spending every day carrying a heavy box around with them. Someday it will happen to all of us.

FIFTH EXERCISE

You will need a pen and a piece of paper for each person at the meeting. Instruct everyone to place their hand on the table – the one they DON'T usually write with. They are to curl the thumb under so that it is touching the palm, and curl the ends of the fingers under so the nails are touching the table. Using the other hand, place the pen so that it is pointed in the direction of the index finger, goes above the little finger, below the ring finger, above the long finger and below the index finger. They are now ready to write. Tell them to write their name on the paper, but don't let their arm rise off the table. Hold the arm still and the wrist stiff, and just use the hand.

Have them hand in the papers and then you will pass them out to the group, so no one has their own paper. Go around the room and let each person read the signatures, if they can. Don't expect neat handwriting.

I want you to remember this exercise and how difficult it was. Remember it the next time you need to have one of your clients sign a paper or a series of papers, and you have to watch them struggle to do something the rest of us take for granted.

SIXTH EXERCISE

This is an exercise to be done off the job. It is too embarrassing to do at work and might lead to a lot of laughter, which would ruin the purpose of the test. Go home and try this with someone close to you. Write down a complete sentence, containing 8 to 10 words, but don't show it to your partner. Now face them and read the sentence. If they can't understand you, read it again, but DON'T change any of the words. Why would they not be able to understand you? Because this test will be performed with you reading while you are holding onto your tongue. Practice that for a few seconds. At the end of this test you will feel the frustration of someone who has great difficulty with their speech and struggles and STRUGGLES to be understood.

SEVENTH EXERCISE

Before you start this exercise, write out the following sentences on a white board or poster board, big enough to be read from the back of the room. Do not show these to the audience until after the exercise.

Also type the sentences out on pieces of paper that can be handed to one of the people in the audience.

Pass out the smaller pieces of paper with the sentences on them and have someone read the following:

1. These are some cities you should visit when you are in Bosnia: Nevesinia, Prijedor, Srebrenica, Zvornik and Bijeljina.

2. There was a time when you heard at least one of these names on the news every night in the early 1960s: Prince Suvanaphoma, Patrice Lumumba, Moises Tshombe, Joseph Kasavubu and Dag Hammerskjold.

After the person has struggled through this, put the first poster board up with these two sentences to show the whole group how difficult these words are. It shows how it feels to have difficulty reading, when even simple words can be as difficult as those above.

Now have someone else read the next two sentences. This time, as the person is reading, instruct the group to listen to them as if this person has a speech problem, and is slow to put words together. Their sentences . . . would have . . . pauses as they . . . struggle to put words together. This could be caused by a brain injury or other developmental disability in clients.

1. These are all professional athletes: Ndamukong Suh, Devin Aramadushu, Dikembe Mutumbo, Zydrunal Ilgauskas and Ikcehuku Ndukwe.
2. If you happen to be in Serbia you might want to visit Sremeska, Mitrovica, Kragujevac and Zrenjanin.

Again, show these last two sentences for all to see after the reading so everyone can see what was just read. Imagine what it would be like to have this much trouble every time you spoke.

When I was 15 years old I passed out in a barber shop and landed on my chin on a concrete floor. The resulting concussion gave me a headache for the next 4 days. I didn't really realize what was happening until school started a couple of weeks later. I raised my hand to answer a question and when called on I completely forgot what I was going to say. This was humiliating for me at the time (lots of things are at that age). This was the beginning of the realization that a brain injury had occurred which was going to affect my speech for the rest of my life. There are times when I am speaking that I must pause in mid-sentence and grasp for the next word. For example, I might say, "The reason your car lights are getting dimmer is ... because your alternator isn't working. I have to pause to formulate the rest of the sentence because my brain can't keep up with what I want to say. This is a frustration that some people with speaking disabilities suffer from on a much larger scale every day of their lives.

This is the end of the tests, but it should be the beginning of you being able to put yourself in the shoes of your clients in a more understanding way. Feeling what they feel will make us all better job coaches. It will create bonds and help us to devise better strategies to help people succeed on the job.

8 - CREW SUPERVISORS ARE JOB COACHES TOO

Do not judge a man until you have walked a mile in his moccasins.

     ____Native American Proverb

Most crew supervisors work in the custodial field and this chapter will address that profession. There are, however some basic principles that apply to all kinds of crews and many that apply to job coaches who work with individuals. So pull up to the table – there is plenty of food here for everyone.

After working with dozens of clients over the years, I have found that everyone I have ever worked with knows something that I don't know. Don't underestimate the abilities that your crew members bring to the table. If you are new to the job you are going to find that, for the most part, your crew will know more than you do. In some cases you will have crew members who have been cleaning these buildings for five years or more.

Learn from your crew, especially in those early days. Spend a lot of time listening, and a lot of time observing. You will get to know the buildings, and more importantly, you will get to know your crew members. You will see their strengths and weaknesses. It will help you to build on those strengths and when possible, to improve on the weaknesses. You are in charge, and responsible for making the decisions, but be a listener, too.

Change is difficult, for both you and your crew. Their previous supervisor probably had a good relationship with them and now you have replaced that person. It is best not to make major changes right away. That's why it is important to listen and gather information before you make changes.

People need time to learn. When you are teaching techniques to a brand new crew member who has not done custodial work before (or a new technique to an established crew member), give them some space. Let them work on it without you standing over them. Some people have delays in their thought processing. They might appear to not understand what you are saying. Don't hurry. Stand back and let the person figure it out. Hovering over them or jumping in to correct them can backfire. Think about this a moment: do you learn best when someone is standing over you? The finished product takes time.

The key to a successful crew is to achieve real teamwork. You will know this is happening when several things occur. For instance, when you encourage it, you will find people helping each other out with their tasks. Or you will find someone saying, "I'm finished, what do you want me to do next?" Finally, as you learn the skill levels that each person possesses, you will give assignments that result in everyone finishing their primary tasks at about the same time.

Achieving teamwork starts with the supervisor. Here's what you do: motivate, motivate, motivate. Each supervisor is different, just as each crew member is different. How you motivate people will come from within yourself, as you use your own individual talents. Understand that each crew member responds differently. Some are motivated by money. If a person is consistently working slower than you know they should be, perhaps a reminder that the combination of working faster and time studies can mean a raise and thus, a bigger paycheck. Getting to know them better often means knowing where they spend their money. Thus, a reminder about taking trips, making a purchase for their home, etc., can act as motivation to work a little faster.

For others, money means absolutely nothing. Someone always seems to pay their bills and provide for other wants and needs so wages are irrelevant. For those persons the main motivation can be the sense of feeling important, wanted, and vital to the crew. When you see someone doing something right, point it out, even if it is some small thing. Positive reinforcement is invaluable. When you can create a few smiles and a positive work atmosphere you will find that people work faster, and with greater quality. Isn't that how all of us react? Emphasize peoples' strengths. They (and we) have enough weaknesses. This is a job and it has to be done right and occasionally you are going to have to correct someone, but use that as a last resort.

This section deals with methods for teaching how to clean. The techniques, however, are good for training for job coaches in lots of situations.

Let's start with rest rooms. Step one is always, "put on latex gloves." This is crucial. I frequently remind folks that they will never get in trouble for using too many gloves. They are inexpensive, disposable, and the best protection against bacteria and disease. A good thing to teach in rest room cleaning is "work from the top down". Do the mirrors first and then the counters and sinks. The same is true with toilets. Where they are floor mounted, you should end at the floor. One of the surest ways to tell that the entire toilet has been thoroughly cleaned is to check the porcelain ledge at the floor. If people are going to take shortcuts it will be found here because bending down and reaching require more effort. You may not see it right away but if toilets are not cleaned clear to the floor, dust and dirt will start to build up and will be noticeable after a few days. Another important emphasis is "use plenty of rags". Depending on the number of fixtures in a given restroom, anywhere from 2 to 5 rags should be used. A soaking wet rag is useless and should be replaced with a dry one. Again, emphasize that no one is going to get in trouble for using too many rags.

Finally, mopping rest rooms or open floors should be done, where possible, in a figure eight motion while walking backwards. It certainly doesn't help to walk where you have already moppcd. You will want to teach mopping that avoids a side to side motion on the rest room floor that can send dirt into the edges and corners where it will build up. Not all of that can be avoided, of course, and sometimes the worker will need to catch these problem areas with a rag and spray bottle. As with so many other things we teach, it is more effective to *show* workers how to do it than it is to *tell* them how to do it.

Collecting trash is similar to cleaning rest rooms. It all starts with wearing latex gloves – no exceptions – to protect the worker. It is not difficult to dump trash for most people. However, if a person's fine motor skills hamper them due to a disability such as cerebral palsy, changing a trash liner can be one of the most difficult tasks in custodial work. It is best to assign a different task to that person, unless they show you that they can do that job. Some people will amaze you in their determination to succeed and to overcome their disability. The word "can't" is not in their vocabulary.

A common temptation is picking up a wastebasket off the floor and setting it on the desk or chair in order to change the liner. People do this because it's easier than bending down to do it. When teaching, be sure to point out that this is unsanitary – a definite no-no.

Teaching vacuuming can be challenging in some cases because our method can run contrary to what a person has observed all their lives. Vacuuming at home usually means cleaning every square foot of open carpet (unless a teenager is asked to do it).

That method has been the norm since Charles Vacuum invented the thing in the first place. We don't have that kind of time. Most contracts call for daily vacuuming and we only vacuum the area where dirt or debris is visible. For some people, especially those who really want to do a perfect job, this idea is foreign and they must be reminded about the way we want it done.

When you are demonstrating vacuuming techniques, it's a good idea to spread some debris on the floor. White dots from a hole puncher are excellent because they are easily seen. Put the dots in one area only and leave the rest of the area alone because it contains no visible debris. Then move the vacuum through the dots (or whatever you are using). Teaching is hard enough under normal conditions. Using a noisy vacuum cleaner can make it harder for some people to hear and understand. Consider doing the initial training with the vacuum turned off. You can move it back and forth across the carpet and also use the wand to demonstrate how to get in small, difficult areas.

Let's take a typical cubicle or office. Vacuum up the obvious dirt, move the chair away from the desk (where dirt likes to hide underneath), and vacuum the vacated area. Now, check under the desk. More often than not you are going to find some computer wires, often with small pieces of debris establishing their new residences in suburban Wiretown. The worker must be shown to keep the head of the vacuum from getting too close to the wires because wires tangled in the vacuum is not good for either the machine or customer relations. Instead, use the wand. That's what it is there for, and you will find that it is your friend. When this is finished be sure to slide the chair back.

Finally, people need to know what *not* to vacuum. You might demonstrate this at the same time that you spread white dots on the floor by adding two of the most common enemies of vacuums everywhere: paper clips and small stones. They should be picked up by hand and discarded. A good rule of thumb is to remember that if something will plug up the machine (like large wads of paper) or will make noise inside the vacuum (coins, paper clips, rocks, etc.) then it shouldn't be vacuumed. And when it comes to safety, point out that you should never run over the vacuum cord or remove the plug from the wall by yanking on the cord.

The most difficult task that I have found to teach is glass cleaning. Job sites often have glass entry doors as well as mirrors that need daily cleaning. When I teach this cleaning technique I emphasize two things.

First, I hold up the spray bottle and say, "this is *not* a fire hose". The meaning is that usually a light spray on a mirror or other glass will do the trick. Secondly, "you are not washing a car". Therefore, it is not necessary to use a circular motion when drying the glass. Use a side to side motion with a rag as you move down the glass and then go around the edges to clean those up. Easy? No, here is where it can get difficult.

Many people have difficulty establishing that side to side motion and revert to either a series of huge "Z's" on the window or some other erratic pattern. Some supervisors have had success using a magic marker type of pen which can be drawn on glass in a back and forth motion which is the same path you would use if you were using a rag. The worker can then use the rag and follow those lines back and forth a few times until they get in the habit of using that motion. Some cannot learn it and others will fall short in some way. Sometimes you just have to accept someone's limitations.

Supervisors are called on to do problem solving, and often in unconventional ways. I once had a crew member who was unable to handle a swivel dust mop. He would get to the end of a floor and instead of swiveling, he left a small dirt pile behind. The object, of course, is to swivel and keep the dirt in front of the dust mop. I solved this by taking a felt pen and drawing a big black arrow on the mop head, showing him to keep that arrow in front of him when he turned the corner. It worked. A couple of weeks later we changed to a mop head without an arrow. By then he had learned and never needed the arrow again. Please, feel free to be unconventional.

Our goal is to support our clients, instruct them as custodians, and to teach proper work habits that apply to employment anywhere. Again, we are trying to create a pleasant work atmosphere, not a boot camp. For instance, how do you give an order, and how is it received?

Example #1: "Vacuum the second floor."

Example #2: "Jim, go ahead and vacuum the second floor. Thanks."

You don't need a doctorate to see that people are going to respond better to Example #2. This is only an example. You will find something that works best for you, something that gives support.

When you are teaching you can say to someone, "Here's how I do it" and then explain why. Some crew member might have a different way. As long as it gets the job done (and in a reasonable amount of time) then I would say let the person do it that way. Certainly, some things are not negotiable, such as wearing protective gloves and vacuuming up car keys. But some methods are acceptable and it is all right to let the person do it their way as long as it is safe.

So what do you do when you have done extensive teaching and someone keeps missing dirt on the floor, forgets to wear gloves, doesn't replace trash liners properly, and generally frustrates the supervisor? Gentle reminders usually work, but what happens when they don't? I have found, as have many athletic coaches and managers, that instead of singling someone out, that it often works better to address the whole crew. I've had problems in the past with people who didn't respond to individual reminders. By calling everyone together I've been able to instruct a whole group in rest room cleaning, for instance, and was able to get my point across to the individual as well as reminding everyone about proper techniques to use on sinks, mirrors, etc. That way I can deliver a message to someone without singling them out and possibly damaging an already fragile self-image. Using a monthly safety meeting is another way of communicating through the use of the group. Make it fun and everyone will learn during such a meeting.

Just as it is with any job, any person, or any situation where a non-disabled person is employed, people have behavioral problems. People start sniping at others, productivity decreases, absenteeism increases, or one person prevents the group from truly working as a team. The same is true for people with disabilities. Somebody is going to have a "bad day." That is normal. When this stretches into several "bad days", then we have to figure out what is wrong. This is why it is crucial to develop a good relationship with the clients that you are serving. Someone once said, "even bad behavior is communication." What is it that your crew member is trying to tell you, and perhaps the whole world?

As noted in a previous chapter the first thing we need to ask is, "what has changed in this person's life?" It could be different work days, different hours, new job duties, changes in medications or need for one, a new caregiver, a death in the family, a new residence, falling in love, or a thousand other things. Sometimes it is as simple as the person not liking their job anymore. Obviously you are not always going to know everything that is happening in a person's life. This is why it is helpful to network and consult with other people who might know the answer. This could include other staff members who know the person, or maybe their caregiver, a relative, etc. By putting our heads together we can often find the answer and solve the problem. Don't be afraid to ask for help.

It happens in every workplace in America. But the quickest way to get to the bottom of a behavioral problem is to know the person by communicating with them and establishing a relationship.

Every friend I make in April is one I will still have in September.

＿＿ John McGraw

McGraw was the manager of the New York Giants baseball team for 30 years. He was referring to the fans of his team over the course of the long season. We would be well served to apply this philosophy to our custodial work. Having a good working relationship with our customers, also known as tenants, is crucial to our program. It helps to smile at people at our job sites, schmooze a little, and spread some good will. The happier you can make the many people who occupy our buildings, the easier everyone's job becomes – especially yours.

Here is why. If the people in the building generally like you, three things will happen. One, the number of complaints will decrease. Two, when there is a reason to complain they often will either handle it gently or ignore it altogether. When we generally do a good job and keep people happy, they will give us a break when we make a mistake, mistakes which are going to happen once in a while. And three, it puts our crew members in a more favorable light. It shows the general public that people with disabilities can do quality work.

Making friends and doing occasional favors will build good relationships. You have to be careful when you do a favor that may not be in the contract. If it is a one time, two minute type of thing, why not do it? Just don't get roped in to being someone's personal attendant. Some people may be difficult and complain about unnecessary things. They will be hard to please. Others are appreciative and never complain. It is the third group sitting on the fence that can be influenced and brought over to your side by your positive attitude and attention to their legitimate needs. Most people are basically good. Don't let a few bad apples cloud your image of the good ones.

Aim high, it's no harder on the rifle.
                              ---Anonymous

When you have both high yet realistic expectations of your crew members, it will amaze you what they can do. Crew supervisors have a definite advantage over job coaches who see an individual only once or twice a week because supervisors spend significantly more time each week with the clients they serve. This is a real boost in getting to know your crew, finding their strengths and weaknesses, and finding ways for each crew member to achieve things that they (and others) didn't think they could do.

I once got the idea in my head that one of my crew members might have the ability to operate a floor buffer. I asked him if he wanted to learn how and he responded, "Yes". In less than ten minutes he had learned. While this was going on another crew member came in and asked if he could learn, also. He did. A third person came along with the same request. She learned, too. In less than one shift three people had learned a marketable skill. I aimed high, but they aimed higher.

You can create an atmosphere where people increase their skills and elevate their self-image at the same time. Positive reinforcement is a vital tool in all this. Treating people as adults – as equals – is a necessity. When you speak to someone, use your normal tone of voice. The mistake occurs when you talk to someone as if they were a child. How can we expect people to step up to the next level when we are talking down to them as if they are already on a lower level? The habit of using an adult conversational tone of voice will establish that equality mentioned above. And on those marvelous days when everything is working smoothly you will sometimes find yourself forgetting that your crew has disabilities. I promise that you will cherish those moments.

Here is one last thing, and probably the most important thing that I can leave with you. Years ago I was given an assignment to work with a group of clients at a laundry where hospital gowns and wash cloths were cleaned. My crew of three clients included a woman who was deaf and spoke only in sign language. I didn't know even one sign. So during my training I approached the supervisor who was well trained in sign language. I wanted her to teach me my first words. The term I first wanted to know was "thank you". Again, I give you my personal guarantee – GUARANTEE – that the more you speak those two words, or something similar, the more cooperation you will get, the faster people will work, the better job they will do, the more their self-image will improve, the more teamwork you will observe, and the more smiles you are going to see.

Oh, and the happier and more fulfilled you will be.

Try it. Thanks... thank you... I appreciate it...

9 – THE JOB COACH EYE EXAM

Look at the chart and tell me what you see.

_ Your local optometrist

Each of us has a group of very vivid memories that we carry with us. They are so vivid that they are easily recalled and thought about frequently, even though they may have occurred years and years ago.

When I was five years old my mother took me on the bus to a soda fountain several blocks away. She ordered a hot fudge sundae for each of us. I had never had one before but I figured that if it had ice cream and chocolate in it, I certainly couldn't go wrong. I was correct in my assessment of the situation. Delicious! I also made a discovery which would repeat itself many times over the next 50 years. As I ate my way down to near the bottom of the dish, I found that the ice cream was gone,

BUT THE HOT FUDGE WASN'T! A happy memory to be sure. Unfortunately, diabetes came along a few years ago and spoiled the party, and all future parties.

I mentioned earlier that my childhood revolved around baseball and the Milwaukee Braves. I loved to play baseball, I loved to talk about baseball, I like to collect baseball cards, I liked to listen to it on the radio and I liked to go see the games. I love baseball. A trip to the ballpark meant riding the street car or the bus, chasing balls in the stands during batting practice, yelling myself silly during the game and getting players' autographs after the game. You can't expend all this energy on an empty stomach, so I used my spending money to buy peanuts and hot dogs. For those of you who are taking notes, my personal best was 8 hot dogs during a double header. Hey, I was eleven years old and weighed about 80 pounds. A young boy's gotta do what a young boy's gotta do. You can see by my comments throughout the book about asparagus, broccoli, blueberry pie, ice cream, hot fudge, peanuts and hot dogs that I am all about nutrition. And when it comes to baseball, I am all about those wonderful memories of baseball in the 1950s. I remember even the smallest incidents which remain vivid in my mind.

The 1960s meant my first decade of adulthood. It was during that time that all three of my children were born. I vividly remember the events of those three days: where I was, what I did, the announcement, ('it's a girl, it's a boy, it's a girl"), no ultra sound then, and my first sight of each baby. Child birth is a time of such hope, a time of strong, happy memories.

It helps me to have memories which aid me in my profession. One in particular stands out. In the 1980s I watched a Made for TV movie called "Nobody's Child" starring Marlo Thomas. It was a good movie, and I thought about it from time to time over the years. It deals with mental illness. I was not involved in human services at the time, so it did not have an immediate impact on me, but I remembered it. More than 20 years later I was having a discussion with a couple of colleagues about a certain client when I brought up the subject of this movie. I decided to purchase a copy of it and watched it again. I was not disappointed.

Let me make a point here. If you will watch this movie I GUARANTEE that you will become a better job coach. It is the true story of Marie Balter, a woman who was committed to a mental health facility as a teen and institutionalized for twenty years. She was mis-diagnosed and over medicated so badly that she could no longer walk or talk A female psychiatrist and a nurse finally took an interest in her. The psychiatrist begged her superior to let her handle Marie's case. The man in charge resisted, and stated that nothing could be done for Marie. Then the psychiatrist made her final plea, "I don't think that she's hopeless. I look in Marie's eyes and I see someone there." The man relented and gave the new psychiatrist the case, and real progress for Marie Balter had begun. I won't give away the rest of the plot because I REALLY want you to watch the movie. You would be wise to have some tissues handy when viewing it.

Going back to that final plea, I must tell you that I can't get it out of my head. I think of it often as I work with my clients.

"I look in Marie's eyes and I see someone there." It is cemented in my memory, in that special section where strong memories live. I wonder how this statement and the movie is going to affect you.

Do you have a client that fits the following description? She misses her appointments, her life at home is a mess, she has difficulty following instructions and does not present well in an interview, has poor hygiene and is disagreeable.

Do you look in her eyes and see someone there?

Another man cannot speak, has trouble walking, has great anxiety, dresses poorly and has failed on every job he has ever had.

Do you look in his eyes and see someone there?

A third lady has no trouble speaking, but great difficulty stopping. She is loud, often insulting or inappropriate and makes others uncomfortable in public. She cannot read, write or count.

Do you look in her eyes and see someone there?

Do you see who these persons seem to be or do you see what they can become?

Every once in a while, a good job coach needs an eye exam.

10 - **DISABLED DOES NOT MEAN UNABLE**

Nothing is impossible.   The impossible just
takes a little longer   ____ Frank

Frank was born in 1902 in Pennsylvania,
one of eight children of Polish immigrants.
As was common at that time, he did not
finish school and went through life with only
an eighth grade education. He did odd jobs
for the next five years to help out the family
and managed to save a little money for
himself.   At the age of 19 he and a friend
struck out on their own and went to work in
the oil fields of Wyoming. Two years later he
left with a lot of mechanical knowledge and
experience, plus $2,000.00 in his bank
account.   He was on his way.   It was the
Roaring Twenties and he was prospering
right along with everyone else.

He became an iron worker, helping to build skyscrapers. He made high wages and started to invest his money. One day he was working twenty stories up next to a friend of his. Frank turned away to grab a wrench and when he turned back his friend was gone. Frank looked down and saw his friend falling to his death. When an accident like this happens everyone is sent home for the rest of the day. The foreman told Frank and the rest of the crew to come back the next day. Frank replied, "I'm not coming back", and he never did.

It was time to find a safer way to make a living. Frank got a construction job, something much safer, dismantling old buildings. He started thinking about more than just himself. He had met a woman he would later marry. In the year leading up to their marriage he built a house for them to move into after the wedding. He got it all done by their wedding day in November of 1928. Well, the house was almost done – he ran out of time and was unable to finish installing a series of electrical switches.

Frank was a man who loved gadgets. Each of these switches performed one convenience or another. For instance, he could flip a switch in the bedroom upstairs when he woke up in the morning and it would turn on the coffeepot downstairs. By the time he was showered and dressed the coffee would be ready. Failure to complete these switches would become important later on – as only Frank knew how the switches worked.

So Frank got married and they went on a three week honeymoon. He returned to work the next Monday morning. He and another man were carrying a large piece of sheet metal and walked past a live wire which was supposed to have been turned off. As they approached, the arc jumped from the wire to the sheet metal. Over 30,000 volts of electricity was involved and caused an explosion, throwing both men across the work area. The two men were rushed to the hospital. Frank lost his left arm below the elbow and one of his legs below the knee. Gangrene set in and he would soon lose the other leg, also below the knee.

The other man had died and Frank was in critical condition and in and out of a coma for the next three weeks. He was barely alive, yet he hung on to life. Whether in a coma or during short periods of consciousness, Frank's mind went back to his new house: "I've got to get those switches installed". Later on he realized that this thought was the one thing that kept him alive. That determination to accomplish this would define him for the rest of his life.

When he came out of the coma for the last time and he was lucid, the reality of his situation began to sink in. He needed two artificial legs and an artificial arm. His remaining arm, his right one was also damaged. His thumb was gone and his four fingers would be permanently stiff. His doctors told him that they could move the fingers into a claw-like position which would at least allow him to pick up some objects and make the hand more useful. Frank consented.

To demonstrate how this looks, lay your hand flat on your thigh. Now curl your thumb under your hand so that it is lying against your palm. It would appear that you have no thumb. Next, curl your four fingers under your hand until the finger nails are touching the thumb. Now pretend the thumb isn't there. That is what Frank's hand looked like. Remember the exercise from the training sessions in a previous chapter when I had your try to write your name? That was how Frank had to sign his name.

In 1928 when a person had injuries this serious the victim was usually put to bed and waited on the rest of their life. Frank would have none of that. He was determined to be as independent as possible. Someone would always have to get him dressed – this would never change. But he taught himself to shave, take a bath and eat and drink. Devices, other than limbs, to assist people with handicaps were either in their infancy or unheard of at this time, so Frank set about inventing his own gadgets.

He had two one inch metal loops welded to the top of the handle of a fork and a spoon. The loops slipped over the ends of his bent fingers and that is how he ate. He could weave the handle of the silverware in and out of his fingers as he did with a pencil, if there were no special pieces of silverware available, as in a restaurant.

He had a flexible goose neck lamp assembly attached permanently to his desk. The light and the electric cord was removed and replaced with a phone cord and a receiver which was adjusted so that it was at the height of his mouth and ear. He would swing the device up to the side of his face when talking on the phone, then push it away at the end of the conversation. Having it permanently attached to the desk kept it from sliding around when he used it, since he couldn't hold things very well with his hand. His home was always full of his gadgets, today known as assistive devices. For recreation he learned to pilot his own boat. He would climb in, grab the handle of the rope on the outboard motor between his first two fingers, pull the rope on the motor and take off. Because of his artificial legs his balance was not as good as it had been before the accident so he had to be more careful while in the boat.

After he got his new arm and legs and had learned to walk, he had a visit from his 17 year old sister. She came into the house and set her car keys on the table. They later walked outdoors and stood chatting next to the car. Frank said to her, "Let's go for a ride." This was wonderful, her big brother wanted to see her drive for the first time since she got her license. So she went to the house to get the keys and returned to the car, only to find Frank sitting behind the wheel. She panicked. She was afraid to tell her big brother he couldn't drive because of his disability, and afraid to ride with him if she gave him the keys. She chose to put the key in the ignition for him and held her breath. Somehow Frank started the car, pushed in the clutch (there were no automatic transmissions in 1929) and took off down the street. Plus he had to use the gear shift lever every time he needed to change gears. This incident in learning how to drive again and getting another driver's license would change not only Frank's life, but later on, the lives of other people with disabilities.

So now he could drive. Not only was this a boost to his self-esteem but it would also allow him make a living. He took his insurance settlement and started a business selling artificial limbs to amputees. He would do this for the next 20 years, and then sold insurance for another fifteen. He could do these things because he could drive and because he was determined to succeed.

In order to drive by himself he had to learn some techniques and invent some things. First, how to steer the car. He figured out a method of using his right hand to rest on the steering wheel in the lower palm area and use the artificial arm to add balance to the whole operation. It worked for him. Cranking the wheel while turning was an effort, but he solved that by putting the outside of his right hand on the inside bar of the steering wheel which, when the wheel is straight, would be in the 3 o'clock position. Try this. Push the steering wheel counterclockwise to the 9 o'clock position, or however far you can crank the wheel. Do NOT use your fingers. Try doing this when you parallel park, back out of an angled or perpendicular parking space, or have to make a one hundred eighty degree back and forth turnaround on a standard size road. No cheating – just use your right hand. And remember, Frank did not have the luxury of power steering in 1929. It had not been invented yet, either.

In case you were wondering how in the world he got the key in the ignition, he had another invention. It was a custom in those days for a gentleman to have a key or two placed in a small leather sheath which had a small rivet inside on which you could hook the keys. You placed the key on the rivet as you would today on a key ring. It was carried in your suit coat or pants pocket. Frank used this leather sheath to solve his car problem.

First he had the sheath attached to one end of a shoestring or similar material and the other end was tied to his front belt loop. He couldn't tie the string to his belt loop, that was part of the job of the person dressing him in the morning. The string was just long enough so it went neatly from belt loop to his pocket when he wasn't driving, but could reach the ignition when needed. When he got behind the wheel he reached down and with a gnarled finger would grab the string, pull the key in the sheath out of his pocket and never have to worry about dropping the key. If he lost his grip on the string or key it could be retrieved easily by grasping the string again. So now he had the key out and got it between his index and middle fingers. The sheath makes it rigid so he can both put it in the ignition and twist it to start the car.

To his detriment he also learned to use the cigarette lighter when they started appearing on the dashboards. He used the same two fingers for the lighter.

When he would meet with potential customers in his office or in their homes he needed a way to show them the articles that he was selling. He would bring a leather case with him which contained a three ring binder filled with plastic pages containing 8"x12" leaflets of whatever he was selling. He couldn't grip the leaflets because of his disability so when he made a presentation he would carry the leather case in under his arm, place it on a desk or table across from his client, unzipped it (he had a string attached to the zipper too) and began to turn the pages one at a time. With what?

Well here's the story. You already read about some of this in the chapter "Training Sessions", the part about writing your name without using your thumb, and having your fingers curled under. Frank would have some pencils with good erasers in his case and he would choose one. He laid it on the desk or table and put his artificial left arm on the eraser end to hold it still while he slipped his fingers (one over, one under, one over, one under) onto the other end of the pencil – the end we would usually sharpen.

This sounds backwards, but the eraser end was the end he needed for this.

By using the eraser he could "grip" the plastic pages and turn them to the next leaflet. He used the same technique for dialing the telephone. (Do each of you know what an old rotary dial telephone was?) By gripping the pencil he would insert the eraser end into the rotary dial to turn it and dial the number he was calling. By gripping a pen in the same way, but with the ink part pointing towards the paper, he could sign his name to a document.

History will never know how Frank thought of these things or how much trial and error and practice it took him to learn to use them. It is enough that he made the effort to learn.

At the end of World War II, beginning in 1946, General Motors was giving away specially equipped Oldsmobiles to veterans who had either lost limbs or were paralyzed in battle. The cars had levers on the dashboard instead of pedals on the floorboard. The only requirement for getting one of the specially equipped cars was for the disabled veteran to get a driver's license.

Frank heard about this and advertised his services. He would travel to anywhere in the state and teach war veterans how to drive – no charge.

When interviewed by the state's largest newspaper, he stated, "I want to help every such person to learn to drive, but if a man lacks ambition there is no power on earth that can help him".

Frank was my father.

We were not as close as a father and son should be. My parents were divorced when I was seven and for a while I saw him only twice a month and later, only twice a year. As I grew up our values would come to differ more and more. Our only common interest was baseball and that provided a lot of bonding.

It was only in the years after he died in 1967, when I was 22, that I began to realize what his life really meant. He left me with a desire to never quit, to never give up. This has kept me going through a lot of difficult times in my life.

His example has also made me a better job coach. It helps me to see inside of a person, to look past the disability and see what talents people have – what they CAN do, not what they can't.

The best lesson I learned from his life is that people with disabilities can work and they can succeed in their work place. Frank wanted what other people wanted. He wanted to do what other people did. He wanted to have what other people had.

Isn't this the desire of everyone who has any type of disability?

ABOUT THE AUTHOR

Don Bayne has worked in Human Services for about 20 years in California and Washington. He started his career in Human Services in a Sheltered Workshop, has provided residential support and worked as a custodial crew supervisor and a job coach.

Born in Wisconsin, he has also lived in Alaska, Texas, Kansas, southern, central and northern California and Washington. He began his college education in Wisconsin and completed it in Kansas and California.

His main hobby is collecting vintage baseball cards and baseball gloves from his childhood days, and before. He also enjoys reading the rich history of baseball, and has a great interest in American History and politics.

He currently lives in Bellingham, WA with his wife JoAnn, near their two daughters and families; their son and his family live in West Virginia. The Baynes have three grandsons, Jahn-Zyel, Ben, and Donnie.

Contact the author at

donbaynejobcoaching@gmail.com